ADDING

Please visit our web site at: www.garethstevens.com
For a free color catalog describing Gareth Stevens Publishing's
list of high-quality books and multimedia programs, call
1-800-542-2595 (USA) or 1-800-387-3178 (Canada).
Gareth Stevens Publishing's fax: (414) 332-3567.

Library of Congress Cataloging-in-Publication Data available upon request from publisher.
Fax (414) 336-0157 for the attention of the Publishing Records Department.

ISBN 0-8368-4108-5

This North American edition first published in 2004 by
Gareth Stevens Publishing
A World Almanac Education Group Company
330 West Olive Street, Suite 100
Milwaukee, WI 53212 USA

Original copyright © 1995 by Creative Teaching Press, Inc.
First published in the United States in 1995 as *Little Number Stories: Addition*
in the *Learn to Read – Read to Learn Math Series* by Creative Teaching
Press, Inc., P.O. Box 2723, Huntington Beach, CA 92647-0723.

Gareth Stevens series editor: Dorothy L. Gibbs
Gareth Stevens series designer: Kami M. Koenig

Printed in the United States of America

1 2 3 4 5 6 7 8 9 08 07 06 05 04

ADDING

Written by Rozanne Lanczak Williams
Photographed by Michael Jarrett

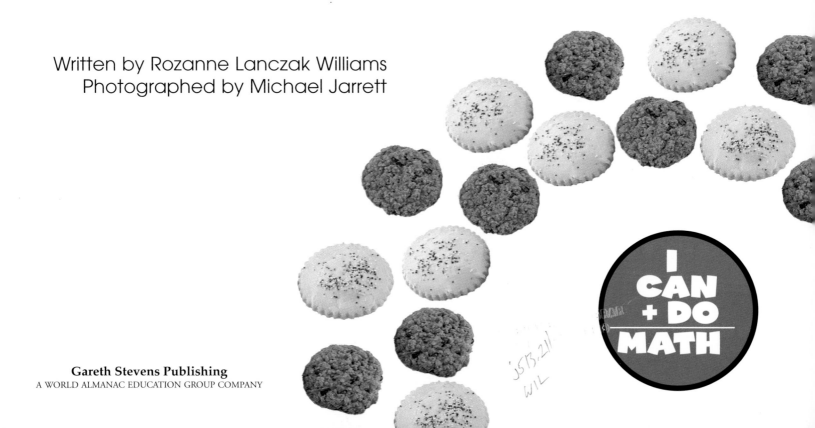

Gareth Stevens Publishing
A WORLD ALMANAC EDUCATION GROUP COMPANY

I
CAN
+ DO
MATH

If you have five apples and five oranges,

how many pieces of fruit do you have?

You have ten pieces of fruit.

$$5 + 5 = 10$$

If you have

six cookies

and

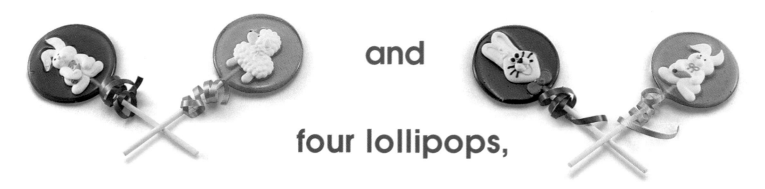

four lollipops,

how many yummy treats do you have?

You have ten yummy treats.

6 + 4 = 10

If you have

five cars,

   three trucks,

and two airplanes,

how many fun toys do you have?

You have ten fun toys.

$$5 + 3 + 2 = 10$$

If you have

four red balls,

four yellow balls,

and two green balls,

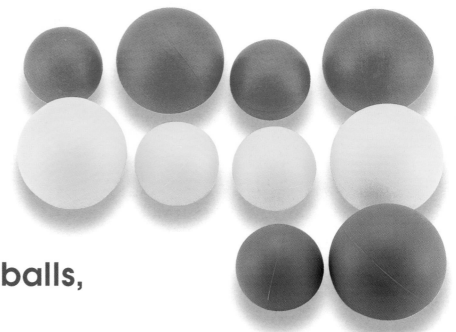

how many colorful balls do you have?

You have ten colorful balls.

$4 + 4 + 2 = 10$

If you have ten happy children

and zero sad children, what do you have?

You have ten happy children.

$$10 + 0 = 10$$

If you have ten pieces of fruit,

1 2 3 4 5 6 7 8 9 10

ten fun toys,

1 2 3 4 5 6 7 8 9 10

ten colorful balls,

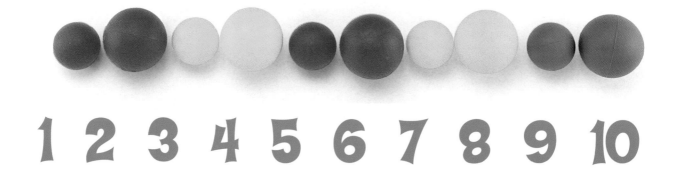

ten yummy treats, and ten happy children,

what do you have?

10 + 10 + 10 + 10 + 10 =

17

A lot of fun!

19

20

Yippee!

Go back and read this book, again,
to see how many numbers add up to . . .

MATH QUIZ (answers on page 24)

1. If you have

one apple,

two lollipops,

three oranges,

and four cookies,

A. how many good things do you have to eat?
B. how many different kinds of foods do you have?

22

2. If you have two balls,

   three trucks,

and five cars,

A. how many fun toys do you have?
B. how many different kinds of toys do you have?

Answers:

1. **A.** $1 + 2 + 3 + 4 = 10$
   B. 4

2. **A.** $2 + 3 + 5 = 10$
   B. 3